S0-AZX-446

THE SEVEN LAST WORDS

BY

FULTON J. SHEEN, Ph.D., D.D. LL.D.

*Agrégé en Philosophie, University of Louvain
and The Catholic University of America*

Martino Publishing
Mansfield Centre, CT
2016

Martino Publishing
P.O. Box 373,
Mansfield Centre, CT 06250 USA

ISBN   978-1-61427-976-1

© *2016 Martino Publishing*

All rights reserved. No new contribution to this publication may
be reproduced, stored in a retrieval system, or transmitted, in any form or
by any means, electronic, mechanical, photocopying, recording, or otherwise,
without the prior permission of the Publisher.

Cover Design Tiziana Matarazzo

Printed in the United States of America On 100% Acid-Free Paper

THE SEVEN LAST WORDS

BY

FULTON J. SHEEN, Ph.D., D.D. LL.D.

*Agrégé en Philosophie, University of Louvain
and The Catholic University of America*

GARDEN CITY BOOKS

Garden City, New York

GARDEN CITY BOOKS REPRINT EDITION 1952, by
special arrangement with Appleton-Century-Crofts, Inc.

COPYRIGHT, 1933, BY THE CENTURY CO.
ALL RIGHTS RESERVED, INCLUDING THE
RIGHT TO REPRODUCE THIS BOOK, OR
PORTIONS THEREOF, IN ANY FORM

PRINTED IN THE UNITED STATES
AT THE COUNTRY LIFE PRESS, GARDEN CITY, N.Y.

Compassionate Queen of the Seven Swords in
Hearts where Christ thy Son is King,
I give thee Seven Words.
Lovingly accept for what is best in them,
Dropped from a cross and the lips of God.

INTRODUCTION

THREE elements conspire in the making of every great message: a pulpit, an audience, and a truth. These three were present in the two most notable messages in the life of Our Blessed Saviour, the first and the last which He delivered to mankind. The pulpit of His first message was the mountainside; His audience, unlettered Galileans; His truth, the Beatitudes. The last message He delivered had for its pulpit the Cross; for its audience, Scribes and Pharisees who blasphemed, temple priests who ridiculed, Roman soldiers who gambled, timid disciples who feared, Magdalen who wept, John who loved, and Mary who grieved as only a mother can grieve. Magdalen, John, and Mary—penitence, priesthood, and innocence—the three types of souls to be found forever beneath the Cross of Christ. The sermon that audience heard from the pulpit of the Cross was the Seven

Last Words, the dying sayings of a Saviour Who, by dying, slew death.

In the four thousand years of Jewish history, the dying words of only three are recorded: Israel, Moses, and Stephen. The reason perhaps is that no others are found so significant and representative as these three. Israel was the first of the Israelites; Moses, the first of the legal dispensation; Stephen, the first martyr. The dying words of each begin something sublime in the history of God's dealings with men. Not even the last words of Peter or Paul or John have been our legacy, for no spirit ever guided a pen to reveal the secrets of their dying lips. And yet the human heart is always anxious to hear of the state of a mind at that very common and yet very mysterious moment called death.

In His goodness, Our Blessed Lord has left us His thoughts on dying, for He more than Israel, more than Moses, more than Stephen is representative of all humanity. In this sublime hour, therefore, He calls all

His children to the pulpit of the Cross, and every word He says to them is set down for the purpose of an eternal publication and an undying consolation. There was never a preacher like the dying Christ. There was never a congregation like that which gathered about the pulpit of the Cross. There was never a sermon like the Seven Last Words.

Those seven words, unlike the words of dying men, never died. They were caught up in the ears of that vast audience and then echoed down over the hillside of Jerusalem and through the labyrinth of men's minds, waking even the dead from their graves. Now even in this hour they are caught up by our own poor hearts that must decide, once more, if they will be tempted by the love of that Saviour. Calvary is the new mountain of temptation, and it is not now Satan tempting Christ, but Christ tempting us—tempting us to love the Love we fall just short of in all love.

CONTENTS

The First Word

FATHER, FORGIVE THEM
FOR THEY KNOW NOT
WHAT THEY DO!

The First Word

FATHER, FORGIVE THEM
FOR THEY KNOW NOT
WHAT THEY DO!

IT SEEMS to be a fact of human psychology
that when death approaches, the human
heart speaks its words of love to those
whom it holds closest and dearest. There is
no reason to suspect that it is otherwise in
the case of the Heart of hearts. If He spoke
in a graduated order to those whom He
loved most, then we may expect to find in
His first three words the order of His love
and affection. His first words went out to
enemies: "Father, forgive them," His second to sinners: "This day thou shalt be
with Me in Paradise," and His third to
saints, "Woman, behold thy son." Enemies, sinners, and saints—such is the

3

order of Divine Love and Thoughtfulness.

The congregation anxiously awaited His first word. The executioners expected Him to cry, for every one pinned on the gibbet of the Cross had done it before Him. Seneca tells us that those who were crucified cursed the day of their birth, the executioners, their mothers, and even spat on those who looked upon them. Cicero tells us that at times it was necessary to cut out the tongues of those who were crucified, to stop their terrible blasphemies. Hence the executioners expected a cry but not the kind of cry that they heard. The Scribes and Pharisees expected a cry, too, and they were quite sure that He who had preached "Love your enemies," and "Do good to them that hate you," would now forget that Gospel with the piercing of feet and hands. They felt that the excruciating and agonizing pains would scatter to the winds any resolution He might have taken to keep up appearances. Every one expected a cry, but no one with the exception of the

4

three at the foot of the Cross, expected the cry they did hear. Like some fragrant trees which bathe in perfume the very axe which gnashes them, the great Heart on the Tree of Love poured out from its depths something less a cry than a prayer, the soft, sweet, low prayer of pardon and forgiveness: "Father, forgive them, for they know not what they do."

Forgive whom? Forgive enemies? The soldier in the court-room of Caiaphas who struck Him with a mailed fist; Pilate, the politician, who condemned a God to retain the friendship of Cæsar; Herod, who robed Wisdom in the garment of a fool; the soldiers who swung the King of Kings on a tree between heaven and earth—forgive them? Forgive them, why? Because they know what they do? No, because they know not what they do. If they knew what they were doing and still went on doing it; if they knew what a terrible crime they were committing by sentencing Life to death; if they knew what a perversion of justice it was to choose Barabbas to Christ; if they knew what cruelty it was to take the feet that trod everlasting hills and pinion them to the limb of a tree; if they knew what they were doing and still went on doing it, unmindful of the fact that the very blood which they shed was capable of redeeming them, they would never be saved! Why, they would be damned if it were not for the fact that they were ignorant of the terrible thing they did when they crucified Christ! It was only the ignorance of their great sin that brought them within the pale of the hearing of that cry from the Cross. It is not wisdom that saves: it is ignorance!

There is no redemption for the fallen angels. Those great spirits headed by the Bearer of Light, Lucifer, endowed with an intelligence compared with which ours is but that of a child, saw the consequences of each of their decisions just as clearly as we see that two and two make four. Having made a decision, they made it irrevocably;

6

there was no taking it back, and hence there was no future redemption. It is because they knew what they were doing that they were excluded from the hearing of that cry that went forth from the Cross. It is not wisdom that saves: it is ignorance!

In like manner, if we knew what a terrible thing sin was and went on sinning; if we knew how much love there was in the Incarnation and still refused to nourish ourselves with the Bread of Life; if we knew how much sacrificial love there was in the Sacrifice of the Cross and still refused to fill the chalice of our heart with that love; if we knew how much mercy there was in the Sacrament of Penance, and still refused to bend a humble knee to a hand that had the power to loose both in heaven and on earth; if we knew how much life there was in the Eucharist and still refused to take of the Bread which makes life everlasting and still refused to drink of that Wine that produces and enriches virgins; if we knew of all the truth there is

7

in the Church as the mystical body of
Christ and still turned our backs to it like
other Pilates; if we knew all these things
and still stayed away from Christ and His
Church, we should be lost! It is not wisdom
that saves; it is ignorance! It is only our
ignorance of how good God is that excuses
us for not being saints!

PRAYER

DEAR JESUS! I do not want to know the
wisdom of the world; I do not want to
know on whose anvil snow-flakes are ham-
mered or the hiding-place of darkness or
from whose womb came the ice, or why
the gold falls to the earth earthly, and fire
climbs to the heavens heavenly; I do not
want to know literature and science, or
the four-dimensional universe in which
we live; I do not want to know the length
of the universe in terms of light years; I
do not want to know the breadth of the
earth as it dances about the chariot of the
sun; I do not want to know the heights of

8

the stars, chaste candles of the night; I do not want to know the depths of the sea or the secrets of its watery palace. I want to be ignorant of all these things. I want only to know the length, the breadth, the height and the depth of Thy redeeming Love on the Cross, Sweet Saviour of Men. I want to be ignorant of everything in the world—everything but You, dear Jesus. And then, by the strangest of strange paradoxes, I shall be wise!

The Second Word

THIS DAY THOU SHALT BE
WITH ME IN PARADISE

The Second Word

THIS DAY THOU SHALT BE WITH ME IN PARADISE

THERE is a legend to the effect that when, to escape the wrath of Herod, Saint Joseph and the Blessed Virgin were fleeing into Egypt with the Divine Child, they stopped at a desert inn. The Blessed Mother asked the lady of the inn for water in which to bathe the Babe. The lady then asked if she might not bathe her own child, who was suffering from leprosy, in the same waters in which the Divine Child had been immersed. Immediately upon touching those waters baptized with the Divine Presence, the child became whole. Her child advanced in age and grew to be a thief. He is Dismas, now hanging on the Cross at the right hand of Christ!

13

Whether the memory of the story his mother told him now came back to the thief and made him look kindly on Christ, we know not. It might have been that his first meeting with the Saviour was on the day when his heart was filled with compunction on hearing the story of a certain man that went down from Jerusalem to Jericho and fell among robbers. Perhaps, too, his first intimation that he was suffering with the Redeemer came to him as he turned his tortured head and read an inscription which bore His name, "Jesus"; His city, "Nazareth"; His crime, "King of the Jews." At any rate, enough dry fuel of the right kind gathers on the altar of his soul, and now a spark from the central Cross falls upon it, creating in it a glorious illumination of faith. He sees a Cross and adores a Throne; he sees a condemned Man, and invokes a King: "Lord, remember me when Thou shalt come into Thy Kingdom."

Our Blessed Lord was owned at last!

14

Amidst the clamor of the raving crowd and
the dismal universal hiss of sin, in all that
delirium of man's revolt against God, no
voice was lifted in praise and recognition
except the voice of a man condemned. It
was a cry of faith in Him whom every one
else had forsaken, and it was only the
testimony of a thief. If the son of the widow
of Nain, who had been raised from the
dead, had cried out a word of faith in the
Kingdom of One who was seemingly losing
His Kingdom; if Peter, who on the Mount
of Transfiguration had seen His face shine
like the sun and His garments whiten like
snow, had acknowledged Him; if the blind
man of Jericho whose eyes were opened to
the light of God's sunshine had been
opened anew to proclaim His Divinity, we
should not have been surprised. Why, if
any of these had cried out, perhaps the
timid disciples and friends would have ral-
lied, perhaps the Scribes and Pharisees
would have believed! But at that moment
when death was upon Him, when defeat

15

stared Him in the face, the only one outside the small group at the foot of the Cross to acknowledge Him as Lord of a Kingdom, as the Captain of Souls, was a thief at the right hand of Christ.

At the very moment when the testimony of a thief was given, Our Blessed Lord was winning a greater victory than any life can win, and was exerting a greater energy than that which harnesses waterfalls; He was losing His life and saving a soul. And on that day when Herod and his whole court could not make Him speak, nor all the power of Jerusalem make Him step down from the Cross, nor the unjust accusations of a court-room force Him to break silence, nor a mob crying, "He saved others; Himself He cannot save," bring from His burning lips a retort, He turns to a quivering life beside Him, speaks, and saves a thief: "This day thou shalt be with Me in Paradise." No one before was ever the object of such a promise, not even

16

Moses nor John, not even Magdalen nor
Mary!

It was the thief's last prayer, perhaps
also his first. He knocked once, sought
once, asked once, dared everything and
found everything. When our spirits stand
with John on Patmos, we can see the white-
stoled army in Heaven riding after the
conquering Christ; when we stand with
Luke on Calvary, we see the one who rode
first in that procession. Christ, who was
poor, died rich. His hands were nailed to a
Cross and yet He unlocked the keys of
Paradise and won a soul. His escort into
Heaven was a thief. May we not say that
the thief died a thief, for he stole Paradise?

Oh, what greater assurance is there in
all the world of the mercy of God? Lost
sheep, prodigal sons, broken Magdalens,
penitent Peters, forgiven thieves! Such is
the rosary of Divine forgiveness.

God is more anxious to save us than we
are to save ourselves. There is a story told

17

to the effect that one day Our Blessed Lord appeared to Saint Jerome, saying to him, "Jerome, what will you give Me?" Jerome answered, "I will give you my writings," to which Our Lord replied that it was not enough. "Then," said Jerome, "what shall I give you? My life of penance and mortification?" But the answer was, "Even that is not enough!" "What have I left to give Thee?" cried Jerome. Our Blessed Lord answered, "Jerome, you can give Me your sins."

PRAYER

DEAR Jesus! Your kindness to the penitent thief recalls the prophetic words of the Old Testament: "If your sins be as scarlet, they shall be made as white as snow: and if they be as red as crimson, they shall be white as wool." In your words of forgiveness to the penitent thief, I understand now the meaning of your words: "I am not come to call the just, but sinners. . . . They that are in health need not a physi-

18

cian, but they that are ill." "There shall be
joy in Heaven upon one sinner that doth
penance more than upon ninety-nine just
who need not penance." I see now why
Peter was not made Thy first vicar on
earth until after he had fallen three times,
in order that the Church of which he was
the head might forever understand forgiveness and pardon. Jesus, I begin to see
that if I had never sinned, I never could
call you "Saviour." The thief is not the
only sinner. Here am I! But Thou art the
only Saviour.

The Third Word

WOMAN, BEHOLD THY SON

The Third Word

WOMAN, BEHOLD THY SON

AN ANGEL of light went out from the great white Throne of Light and descended over the plains of Esdraelon, past the daughters of the great kingdoms and empires, and came to where a humble virgin of Nazareth knelt in prayer, and said, "Hail, full of grace!" These were not words; they were the Word. "And the Word became flesh." This was the first Annunciation.

Nine months passed and once more an angel from that great white Throne of Light came down to shepherds on Judean hills, teaching them the joy of a "Gloria in excelsis," and bidding them worship Him Whom the world could not contain, a "Babe wrapped in swaddling clothes and laid in a manger." Eternity became time, Divinity incarnate, God a man; Omnipotence was discovered in bonds. In the language of Saint Luke, Mary "brought forth her first-born Son . . . and laid Him in a manger." This was the first Nativity.

Then came Nazareth and the carpenter shop where one can imagine the Divine Boy, straitened until baptized with a baptism of blood, fashioning a little cross in anticipation of a great Cross that would one day be His on Calvary. One can also imagine Him in the evening of a day of labor at the bench, stretching out His arms in exhausted relaxation, whilst the setting sun traced on the opposite wall the shadow of a man on a cross. One can, too, imagine His Mother seeing in each nail the prophecy and the tell-tale of a day when men would carpenter to a Cross the One who carpentered the universe.

Nazareth passed into Calvary, and the nails of the shop into the nails of human malignity. From the Cross He completed His last will and testament. He had already committed His blood to the Church, His

24

garments to His enemies, a thief to Paradise, and would soon commend His body to the grave and His soul to His Heavenly Father. To whom, then, could He give the two treasures which He loved above all others, Mary and John? He would bequeath them to one another, giving at once a son to His Mother and a Mother to His friend. "Woman!" It was the second Annunciation! The midnight hour, the silent room, the ecstatic prayer had given way to the mount of Calvary, the darkened sky, and a Son hanging on a Cross. Yet, what consolation! It was only an angel who made the first Annunciation, but it is God's own sweet voice which makes the second.

"Behold thy son!" It was the second Nativity! Mary had brought forth her First-born without labor, in the cave of Bethlehem; she now brings forth her second-born, John, in the labors of the Cross. At this moment Mary is undergoing the pains of childbirth, not only for her

25

second-born, who is John, but also for the
millions who will be born to her in Chris-
tian ages as "Children of Mary." Now we
can understand why Christ was called "her
First-born." It was not because she was
to have other children by the blood of flesh,
but because she was to have other children
by the blood of her heart. Truly, indeed,
the Divine condemnation against Eve is
now renewed against the new Eve, Mary,
for she is bringing forth her children in
sorrow.

Mary, then, is not only the Mother of
Our Lord and Saviour, Jesus Christ, but
she is also our Mother, and this not by a
title of courtesy, not by legal fiction, not
by a mere figure of speech, but by the right
of bringing us forth in sorrow at the foot
of the Cross. It was by weakness and dis-
obedience at the foot of the tree of Good
and Evil that Eve lost the title of the
Mother of the Living; it is at the foot of the
tree of the Cross that Mary, by sacrifice and
obedience, regained for us the title of the

Mother of Men. What a destiny to have the Mother of God as my Mother and Jesus as my Brother!

PRAYER

O MARY! as Jesus was born to thee in thy first Nativity of the flesh, so we have been born of thee in thy second Nativity of the spirit. Thus thou didst beget us into a new world of spiritual relationship with God as our Father, Jesus as our Brother, and thou as our Mother! If a mother can never forget the child of her womb, then, Mary, thou shalt never forget us. As thou wert Co-Redemptrix in the acquisition of the graces of eternal life, be thou also our Co-Mediatrix in their dispensation. Nothing is impossible for thee, because thou art the Mother of Him who can do all things. If thy Son did not refuse thy request at the banquet of Cana, He will not refuse it at the celestial banquet where thou art crowned as Queen of Angels and Saints. Intercede therefore to thy Divine Son, that

27

He may change the waters of my weakness into the wine of thy strength. Mary, thou art the Refuge of Sinners! Pray for us, now prostrate at the foot of the Cross. Holy Mary, Mother of God, pray for us sinners, now and at the hour of our death. Amen.

The Fourth Word

MY GOD! MY GOD! WHY
HAST THOU FORSAKEN
ME?

The Fourth Word

MY GOD! MY GOD! WHY
HAST THOU FORSAKEN
ME?

THE first three words from the pulpit of
the Cross were addressed to the three
predilections of God: enemies, sinners,
and saints. The next two words, the fourth
and the fifth, betray the sufferings of the
God-man on the Cross. The fourth word
symbolizes the sufferings of man abandoned by God; the fifth word the sufferings of God abandoned by man.

When Our Blessed Lord spoke this
fourth word from the Cross, darkness cov-
ered the earth. It is a common remark that
nature is indifferent to our griefs. A nation
may be dying of famine, yet the sun starts
and plays upon the stricken fields. Brother

may rise up against brother in a war which turns poppy fields into Haceldamas of blood; yet a bird, safe from the fire and shell, chants its little song of peace. Hearts may be broken by the loss of a friend; yet a rainbow leaps with joy across the heavens, making a terrible contrast between its smile and the agony it shines upon. But the sun refused to shine on the crucifixion! The light that rules the day, probably for the first and last time in history, was snuffed out like a candle when, according to every human calculation, it should have continued to shine. The reason was that the crowning crime of man, the killing of nature's Lord, could not pass without a protest from nature itself. If the soul of God were in darkness, so should be the sun which He had made.

Truly, all was darkness! He had given up His Mother and His beloved disciple, and now God seemingly abandoned Him. "Eli, Eli, lamma sabacthani?" "My God!

32

My God! Why hast Thou forsaken Me?"
It is a cry in the mysterious language of
Hebrew to express the tremendous mys-
tery of a God "abandoned" by God. The
Son calls His Father, God. What a contrast
with a prayer He once taught: "Our Father, Who art in Heaven!" In some
strange, mysterious way His human nature
seems separated from His Heavenly Father, and yet not separated, for otherwise
how could He cry, "My God, My God"?
But just as the sun's light and heat can be
withdrawn from us by the intervening
clouds, though the sun remains in the
sky, so there was a kind of withdrawal of
His Father's Face in the terrible moment
in which He took upon Himself the sins of
the world. This pain and desolation He
suffered for each of us, that we might know
what a terrible thing it is for human nature
to be without God, to be deprived of a Divine Remedy and Consolation. It was the
supreme act of atonement for three classes

of people: those who abandon God, those who doubt the presence of God, and those who are indifferent to God.

He atoned first of all for atheists, for those who on that dark midday half believed in God, as even now at night they half believe in Him. He atoned also for those who know God, but live as if they had never heard His name; for those whose hearts are like waysides on which God's love falls only to be trampled by the world; for those whose hearts are like rocks on which the seed of God's love falls only to be quickly forgotten; for those whose hearts are like thorns on which God's love descends only to be choked by the cares of the world. It was atonement for all who have had faith and lost it; for all who once were saints and now are sinners. It was the Divine Act of Redemption for all abandonment of God, for in that moment in which He was forgotten, He purchased for us the grace of never being forgotten by God.

It was also the atonement for that other

class who deny the presence of God; for all those Christians who abandon all effort when they cannot feel God near them; for all who identify being good with feeling good; for all those skeptics beginning with the first who asked, "Why has God commanded you?" It was reparation for all the haunting questions of a doubting world: "Why is there evil?" . . . "Why does God not answer my prayers?" . . . "Why did God take away my mother?" . . . "why" . . . "why" . . . "why"; and the reparation for all those queries was made when God asked a "why" of God.

Finally, it was atonement for all the indifference of the world which lives as if there had never been a crib at Bethlehem or a Cross at Calvary; it was atonement for all who shake dice while the drama of Redemption is being enacted; for all those who feel themselves as gods beyond all duties of worship and religion, yet bound by none. I suppose that after these twenty centuries the indifference of our modern

35

world is more torturing and crucifying than the pains of Calvary. One can well believe that a crown of thorns, and that steel nails were less terrible to the flesh of our Saviour than our modern indifference which neither scorns nor prays to the Heart of Christ.

PRAYER

JESUS! Thou art now atoning for those moments when we are neither hot nor cold, members neither of heaven nor of earth, for now Thou art suffering between the two: rejected by the one, abandoned by the other. Because Thou wouldst not give up sinful humanity, Thy Heavenly Father hid His Face from Thee. Because Thou wouldst not give up Thy Heavenly Father, sinful humanity turned its back to Thee, and thus in holy fellowship Thou didst unite us both. No longer can men say that God does not know what a heart suffers in abandonment, for now Thou art abandoned. No longer can men complain that

36

God does not know the wounds of an inquiring heart which feels not the Divine Presence, for now that sweet Presence is seemingly hid from Thee. Jesus, now I understand pain, abandonment, and suffering, for I see that even the sun has its eclipse. But Jesus, why do I not learn? Teach me that just as Thou didst not make Thy own Cross, neither shall I make my own, but accept the one Thou makest for me. Teach me that everything in the world is Thine, except one thing, and that is my own will; and since that is mine, it is the only real and true gift that I can ever bestow. Teach me to say, "Not my will, but Thine be done, O Lord." Even when I see Thee not, grant me the grace to believe and "although Thou slayest me, yet will I trust Thee." Tell me, how long, how long, O Lord, will I keep Thee writhing on the Cross?

The Fifth Word

I THIRST

The Fifth Word

I THIRST

THIS is the shortest of the seven cries. Although it stands in our language as two words, in the original it is one. At the moment when Our Saviour resumes His sermon, it is not a curse upon those who crucify Him, not a word of reproach to the timid disciples at the border of the crowd, not a cry of scorn to the Roman soldiers, not a word of hope to Magdalen, not a word of love to John, not a word of farewell to His own mother. It is not even to God at this moment! Out from the depths of the Sacred Heart there wells through parched lips one awful word: "I thirst!"

He, the God-Man, who threw the stars in their orbits and spheres into space, who "swung the earth a trinket at his wrist," from Whose finger-tips tumbled planets

41

and worlds, who might have said, "The sea
is Mine and with it the streams in a thousand valleys and the cataracts in a thousand hills," now asks man—man, a piece
of His own handiwork—to help Him. He
asks man for a drink! Not a drink of
earthly water, that is not what He meant,
but a drink of love. "I thirst"—for love!

The last word was a revelation of the
sufferings of a man without God; this word
was a revelation of the sufferings of a God
without man. The Creator cannot live
without the creature, the Shepherd without the sheep, the thirst of Christ's love
without the soul-water of Christians.

But what has He done to be entitled to
my love? How much has God loved me?
Oh, if I would know how much God has
loved me, then let me sound the depths of
meaning of that word "love," a word so
often used and so little understood. Love,
first of all, means to give and God has given
His power to nothingness, His light to
darkness, His order to chaos, and this is

Creation. Love means to tell secrets to the one loved, and God has told in the Scriptures the secrets of Nature and His high hopes for fallen humanity, and this is Revelation. Love means also to suffer for the one loved, that is why we speak of arrows and darts of love—something that wounds—and God is now suffering for us on the Tree of the Cross, for "greater love than this no man hath, that he lay down his life for his friend." Love means also to become one with the one loved, not only in the unity of flesh but in the unity of spirit, and God has so loved us as to institute the Eucharist, that we may abide in Him and He in us in the ineffable unity of the Bread of Life. Love wishes also to be eternally united with the one loved, and God has so loved us that He has promised us His Father's mansions, where a peace and a joy reign which the world cannot give and time cannot take away, and this is Heaven.

Certainly, love has exhausted itself. There is nothing more that Christ could do for His vineyard than He has done. Having poured forth all the waters of His everlasting Love on our poor parched hearts, it is no wonder that He thirsts for love. If love is reciprocal then certainly He has a right to our love. Why do we not respond? Why do we let the Divine Heart die of the thirst for human hearts? With what justice He might complain:

Lo, all things fly thee, for thou fliest Me!
Strange, piteous, futile thing!
Wherefore should any set thee love apart?
Seeing none but I makes much of naught [He
    said],
And human love needs human meriting:
How hast thou merited—
Of all man's clotted clay the dingiest clot?
Alack, thou knowest not
How little worthy of any love thou art!
Whom wilt thou find to love ignoble thee,
Save Me, save only Me? [1]

PRAYER

DEAR JESUS! Thou hast given all for me, and yet I give nothing in return. How

[1] Francis Thompson, "The Hound of Heaven."

44

often Thou hast come to gather vintage in the vineyard of my soul, and hast found only a few clusters! How often Thou soughtest, and found nothing; knocked, and the door of my soul was closed to Thee! How often Thou didst ask for a drink, and I gave Thee only vinegar and gall!

How often, dear Jesus, I feared lest, having Thee, I must have naught beside. I forget that if I had the flame, I would forget the spark; if I had the sun of Thy love, I could forget the candle of a human heart; if I had the perfect round of Thy happiness, I could forget the broken arc of earth. O Jesus, my story is the sad story of a refusal to return heart for heart, love for love. Give me, above all human gifts, the sweet gift of sympathy for Thee.

Am I a stone and not a sheep
That I can stand, O Christ, beneath Thy Cross
To number drop by drop Thy Blood's slow
    loss,
And yet not weep?

Not so those women loved
Who with exceeding grief lamented Thee;
Not so fallen Peter weeping bitterly;
Not so the thief was moved;

Not so the sun and moon
Which hid their faces in a starless sky,
A horror of great darkness at broad noon
I, only I.

Yet give not o'er,
But seek Thy sheep, true Shepherd of the flock,
Greater than Moses, turn and look once more
And smite a rock.[1]

[1] Christina Rossetti

The Sixth Word

IT IS CONSUMMATED

The Sixth Word

FROM all eternity God willed to make man to the image of His eternal Son. After having painted the heavens with blue and the earth with green, God then made a garden, beautiful as only God knows how to make a garden beautiful, and in it placed man made to conform to the image of God's Son. In some mysterious way the revolt of Lucifer echoed to earth, and the image of God in man was blurred and ruined.

The Heavenly Father in His divine mercy willed to restore man to his pristine glory. In order that the portrait might once more be true to the Original, God willed to send to earth His Divine Son according to whose image man was made, that the earth might see once more the manner of man

49

God wanted us to be. In the accomplishment of this task, only Divine Omnipotence could use the elements of defeat as the elements of victory. In the Divine economy of Redemption, the same three things which coöperated in our fall shared in our redemption. For the disobedient man Adam, there was the obedient man Christ; for the proud woman Eve, there was the humble virgin Mary; for the tree of the garden, there was the tree of the Cross. The Redemption was now completed. The work which His Father had given Him to do was accomplished. We were bought and paid for. We were won in a battle fought not with five stones like those with which David slew Goliath, but with five wounds, hideous scars on hands and feet and side; in a battle fought not with armor glistening under a noonday sun, but with flesh hanging like purple rags under a darkened sky; in a battle where the cry was not "Crush and kill," but "Father, forgive"; in a battle fought not with spitting steel, but with

50

dripping blood; in a battle in which he who slew the foe lost the day. Now the battle was over. For the last three hours He had been about His Father's business. The artist had put the last touch on his masterpiece and with the joy of the strong He uttered the song of triumph: "It is finished."

His work is finished, but is ours? It belongs to God to use that word, but not to us. The work of acquiring Divine life for man is finished, but not the distribution. He has finished the task of filling the reservoir of Calvary's sacramental life, but the work of letting it flood our souls is not yet finished. He has finished the foundation; we must build upon it. He has finished the ark, opening His side with a spear and clothing Himself in the garment of His precious blood, but we must enter the ark. He stands at the door and knocks, but the latch is on the inside, and only we can open it. He has enacted the consecration, but the communion depends upon us; and whether our work will ever be finished depends entirely on how we relive His life and become other Christs, for His Good Friday and His passion avail us nothing unless we take up His Cross and follow Him. Sin is the great obstacle to the accomplishment of that task, for as long as there is sin in the world, Christ is crucified anew in our hearts.

> I saw the Son of God go by
> Crowned with the crown of thorn.
> "Was it not finished, Lord?" I said,
> "And all the anguish borne?"
>
> He turned on me His awful eyes:
> "Hast Thou not understood?
> Lo! Every soul is Calvary,
> And every sin a rood." [1]

PRAYER

DEAR Jesus! redemption is Thy work; atonement is mine, for atonement means at-one-ment with Thy life, Thy truth, and Thy love. Thy work on the cross is finished, but my work is to take you down, for—

[1] Rachel Annand Taylor.

52

Whenever there is silence around me
By day or by night—
I am startled by a cry.
It came down from the cross—
The first time I heard it,
I went out and searched—
And found a Man in the throes of crucifixion,
And I said, "I will take you down,"
And I tried to take the nails out of His feet.
But He said, "Let them be
For I cannot be taken down
Until every man, every woman, and every
    child
Come together to take Me down."
And I said ,"But I cannot bear Your cry.
What can I do?"
And He said, "Go about the world—
Tell everyone that you meet—
There is a Man on the cross." [1]

Thou art on the Cross, but we must take Thee down. Thou hast been hanging there long enough! Through Thy Apostle, Paul, Thou hast told us that those who are Thine crucify their flesh and its concupiscences. My work, then, is not finished until I take Thy place upon the Cross, for unless there

[1] Elizabeth Cheney.

is a Good Friday in my life, there will never be an Easter Sunday; unless there is a garment of a fool, there will never be the white robes of wisdom; unless there is the crown of thorns, there will never be the glorified body; unless there is the battle, there will never be the victory; unless there is the thirst, there will never be the Heavenly Refreshment; unless there is the Cross, there will never be the empty tomb. Teach me, Jesus, to finish this task, for it is fitting that the sons of men should suffer and enter into their glory.

The Seventh Word

FATHER, INTO THY HANDS
I COMMEND MY SPIRIT

The Seventh Word

FATHER, INTO THY HANDS
I COMMEND MY SPIRIT

WHEN Adam had been driven from the Garden of Paradise, and the penalty of labor imposed upon him, he went out in quest of the bread he was to earn by the sweat of his brow. In the course of that search, he stumbled upon the limp form of his son Abel, picked him up, carried him upon his shoulders, and laid him on the lap of Eve. They spoke to him, but Abel did not answer. He had never been so silent before. They lifted his hand, but it fell back limp; it had never acted that way before. They looked into his eyes, cold, glassy, mysteriously elusive; they had never been so unresponsive before. They wondered, and as they wondered, their wonder grew. Then they remembered: "For in what day soever thou shalt eat of the tree, thou shalt die the death." *It was the first death in the world.*

Centuries whirled around into space, and the new Abel, Christ, is put to death by his jealous brethren of the race of Cain. The life that came out from the boundless deep now prepares to return home. His sixth word was a cry of retrospect: "I have finished the work." His seventh and last one is a word of prospect: "I commend My Spirit." The sixth word was man-ward; the seventh word was God-ward. The sixth word was a farewell to earth; the seventh His entrance into Heaven. Just as those great planets only after a long time complete their orbit and return again to their starting-point, as if to salute Him who sent them on their way, so He who had come from Heaven had finished His work and completed His orbit, now goes back to the Father to salute Him who sent Him out on the great work of the world's redemption: "Father, into Thy hands I commend My Spirit."

The Prodigal Son is returning to His Father's house, for is not Christ the Prodigal? Thirty-three years ago He left His Father's eternal mansion and went off into the foreign country of this world. Then He began spending Himself and being spent; dispensing with an infinite prodigality the divine riches of power and wisdom and bestowing with a heavenly liberality the divine gifts of pardon and mercy. In this last hour His whole substance is wasted among sinners, for He is giving the last drop of His precious blood for the redemption of the world. There is nothing to feed upon except the husks of human sneers and the vinegar and gall of bitter human ingratitude. He now prepares to take the road back to His Father's house, and when yet some distance away He sees the face of His Heavenly Father He breaks out into the last and perfect prayer from the pulpit of the Cross: "Father, into Thy hands I commend My Spirit."

All the while Mary is standing at the foot of the Cross. In a short time the new Abel, slain by His brethren, will be taken down from the gibbet of salvation and laid in the lap of the new Eve. It will be the death of Death! But when the tragic moment comes it may seem to the tear-dimmed eyes of Mary that Bethlehem has come back. The thorn-crowned head which had nowhere to lay itself in death, except on the pillow of the Cross, may, through Mary's clouded vision, seem the head which she drew to her breast at Bethlehem. Those eyes at whose fading even the sun and moon were darkened were to her the eyes that glanced up from a crib of straw. The helpless feet riveted with nails once more seem to her the baby feet at which were cast gold, frankincense, and myrrh. The lips now parched and crimsoned with blood seem the ruddy lips that once at

60

Bethlehem nourished themselves on the Eucharist of her body. The hands that can hold nothing but a wound, seem once more the baby hands that were not quite long enough to touch the huge heads of the cattle. The embrace at the foot of the Cross seems the embrace at the side of the crib. In that sad hour of death which always makes one think of birth, Mary may feel that Bethlehem is returning again.

PRAYER

No, MARY! Bethlehem is not come back. This is not the crib, but the Cross; not birth, but death; not the day of companionship with Shepherds and Kings, but the hour of a common death with thieves; not Bethlehem, but Calvary.

Bethlehem is Jesus, as thou, His sinless mother, gave Him to man; Calvary is Jesus, as sinful man gave Him back to thee. Something intervened between Thy giving at the manger and thy receiving at the Cross, and that which intervened is my

61

sins. Mary, this is not thy hour; it is my hour—my hour of wickedness and sin. If I had not sinned, death would not now hover on its black wings about His crimsoned body; if I had not been proud, the atoning crown of thorns would never have been woven; if I had been less rebellious in treading the broad way which leads to destruction, the feet would never have been pierced with nails; if I had been more responsive to His shepherding calls from the thorns and thistles, His lips would have never been on fire; if I had been more faithful, His cheeks would never have been blistered with the kiss of Judas.

Mary, it is I who stand between His birth and His approaching redemptive death. I warn thee, Mary, think not when thy arms come to clasp Him, that He is white as He came from the Father; He is red as He came from me. In a few short seconds thy Son shall have surrendered His soul to His Heavenly Father, and His body to thy caressing hands. The last few drops

62

of blood are falling from that great chalice of Redemption, staining the wood of the Cross and crimsoning the rocks soon to be rent in horror; and a single drop of it would be sufficient to redeem ten thousand worlds. Mary, my Mother, intercede with thy Divine Son for forgiveness of the sin of changing thy Bethlehem into Calvary. Beg Him, Mary, in these last remaining seconds, to grant us the grace of never crucifying Him again nor piercing thy own heart with seven swords. Mary, plead to thy dying Son that as long as I live . . . Mary! Jesus is dead. . . . Mary!

(6)

CPSIA information can be obtained
at www.ICGtesting.com
Printed in the USA
LVHW110755010319
609178LV00006B/116/P

9 781614 279761